The Accidental Candidate

The Accidental Candidate

The Rise and Fall of Alvin Greene

Written by COREY HUTCHINS and DAVID AXE

Art by BLUE DELLIQUANTI

Foreword by William "Jack" Hamilton

McFarland & Company, Inc., Publishers
Jefferson, North Carolina, and London

Much of the information in this book was obtained from personal interviews or firsthand observation. Dialogue is based on interviews with subjects, published reports or recreations of conversations by sources. In instances where no reporter or source was present, such dialogue or events reflect what the authors believe is accurate. Some scenes have been dramatized.

LIBRARY OF CONGRESS CATALOGUING-IN-PUBLICATION DATA

Hutchins, Corey.
The accidental candidate : the rise and fall of Alvin Greene / written by Corey Hutchins and David Axe ; art by Blue Delliquanti ; foreword by William "Jack" Hamilton.
p.   cm.

ISBN 978-0-7864-7429-5
softcover : acid free paper ∞

1. Greene, Alvin, 1977–   2. Political candidates—South Carolina—Biography. 3. African American veterans—South Carolina—Biography. 4. Democratic Party (S.C.)—Biography.   5. United States. Congress. Senate—Elections, 2010.   6. South Carolina—Politics and government—1951. 7. United States—Politics and government—2009–   I. Axe, David.   II. Title.
F275.42.G74H88 2012   975.7'043092—dc23   [B]   2012036844

BRITISH LIBRARY CATALOGUING DATA ARE AVAILABLE

Cover by Dre Lopez

Manufactured in the United States of America

McFarland & Company, Inc., Publishers
Box 611, Jefferson, North Carolina 28640
www.mcfarlandpub.com

Table of Contents

This book was made possible by the Columbia, S.C. *Free Times*, which values long-form, investigative journalism at a time when newsrooms have adopted a model of doing more with less.

Foreword by
William "Jack" Hamilton

History, in South Carolina, is generally an elaborate explanation of what went wrong. Since the Civil War we have preferred our heroes tragic and defeated. Winning embarrasses us.

That was very much on my mind when I and 900 other delegates of the South Carolina Democratic Party convened at the Carolina Coliseum in Columbia for our April 2011 convention.

The previous November, Democrats in the Palmetto State had lost every election for statewide office for the first time in history.

After three decades of service, a fine, intelligent Congressman, John Spratt, had been unseated by a real-estate huckster who lived mere feet from the North Carolina border. Nikki Haley, a no-name reliable shill for neo-libertarian corporate money, had become governor. And Vic Rawl, a good and decent man, a former state legislator who pushed for lobbying reform, a former judge and candidate whom I advised, never even got the chance to challenge Tea Party darling Jim DeMint for the U.S. Senate.

A market research executive, DeMint is the most conservative senator in the country. He had whipped South Carolina's senior Republican senator, Lindsey Graham, into complicity while organizing a money machine to cripple the hope and change promised by Pres. Barack Obama.

DeMint had been sleeping in a Washington, D.C. house belonging to The Family, a secretive and mysterious, uber-connected society of fundamentalist politicians. He preached a fire-breathing hatred of teachers, libraries, parks, artists and homosexuals.

Between that bright morning in 2010 when Rawl announced he would challenge DeMint, and that sad convention of beaten people a year later, something went terribly wrong.

An unemployed, socially awkward, 32-year-old Army veteran from the small town of Manning, a man with no political experience who had been kicked out of the Army and recently been arrested on an obscenity charge, defeated Rawl in the Democratic primary. This troubled young man did not campaign. He did not have a cell phone or a Website. To this day, no one is sure just exactly *how* he won.

His name is Alvin Greene. He was soundly beaten by DeMint in the general election. Greene's rise and fall helped seal South Carolina's fate.

As the South Carolina Democrats convened at the Coliseum in 2011, the walls of moderate political decency were down everywhere in our state. South Carolina's schools, social programs, environment and tax system were fully exposed to the whims of the billionaire Koch brothers and the right-wing think-tank money-machine.

The state's Democratic convention that year was a sad and sobering thing. The delegates were shoehorned into the tight, steeply raked seating of the Coliseum stands. Many were elderly, disabled and obese. They struggled up and down the long stairways, some with canes and oxygen tanks. Once seated, they couldn't move.

My wife went to the restroom and decided not to fight her way back to her assigned seat. She found a block of empty seats and thus became, to any of those who might have looked up, the sole occupant of the block of seating assigned to the Democrats of Allendale County.

Allendale is one of the sickest, poorest, and most geriatric counties in South Carolina, abandoned by everyone who can escape. It's almost completely dependent on a prison and government handouts for its economy. Nowhere needs the Democrats more than Allendale. However, the Democrats had failed to offer enough hope and change to motivate anyone who lived there to make the 60-mile trip to Columbia that day.

After some debate, the rules committee slyly called for a change. It wanted easily-manipulated voice voting for party offices instead of the traditional paper ballots. To beat this dangerous measure required a "yes" vote on a motion to table an amendment to return the party convention to voice voting for offices. A "yes" vote to say "no" to an un-democratic change. Confusion and frustration rippled across the room. Civics is barely taught in South Carolina.

My son had been elected to a high-school student council where parliamentary procedure was never used, half of the representatives were appointed by the faculty, there were no votes, and the election for student body president was uncontested. Politics in the state generally consists of working for your friends and getting favors later.

I had seen enough, heard enough and felt enough rage and frustration at the convention and over the previous year. If we don't stop it, starting here and now, South Carolina's political disease may infect the nation.

I rose to my feet in the vast, dim Coliseum. I am a loud man. Still, I was startled when the sound of my protest echoed off the walls. When the vote came, I yelled, "Stand up for verifiable votes!" Seven hundred people rose with me, the weary survivors of it all, still demanding votes that mattered.

As pathetic as we might have seemed, the tired Democrats of South Carolina in 2011 were fighting to buy time for the United States of America. Time to wake up. Time to make things right.

Since then the contagion that Alvin Greene may have been a symptom of has continued to erupt across the Republic. In 2012, a right-wing redneck conspiracy theorist won the Democratic nomination for the U.S. Senate in Tennessee and was disowned by state Democrats, turning the race into a spectacle comparable to that of Alvin Greene.

Massive manipulations attended the 2012 GOP presidential primaries. The Iowa caucuses went to Mitt Romney when Rick Santorum had actually won, and later Ron Paul got the delegates. Herman Cain, a rich man's Alvin Greene with pizza on his resume, had been inflated by money and burst like a rotten balloon in a matter of weeks. Ken Ard, South Carolina's lieutenant governor, who didn't even bother to register to vote until he was 40, was forced from office after being indicted on public corruption charges following an elaborate campaign-finance scheme. Gov. Haley survived several embarrassing pay-to-play ethics scandals and accusations that she'd illegally lobbied as a lawmaker on the miserable defense that everyone in South Carolina was doing it.

In Zuccotti Park in New York City, Occupy Wall Street rose up like a Twitter-enabled

Foreword by William "Jack" Hamilton

flashmob, spread across the country, and shredded itself in three months on the realities of a nation that can apparently no longer plan, manage or tolerate a protest march.

Like Alvin Greene blinking at himself on television from his living room, the competence and sustained discipline to wage effective politics seems to be slipping from the grasp of American citizens.

Amid national politics of balkanized extremism, huge dumps of incompetence, cynicism and hopelessness have spread in the way that the pine barrens of New Jersey once accumulated rusting drums of toxic waste, dispatched by greed and transported by corruption. Unknown billionaires write the checks. Some dumps are the abandoned places of the losers. Others are the fortified reserves of those who have won. Ugly, mutated things escape from both. The surrounding landscape is no longer ecologically healthy enough to sustain the competition and awareness to end or contain them.

This book is a warning. Alvin Greene's political "career" is a symptom of an inherited weakness in the American Republic. The politics of money and fear is metastasizing into a national cancer that could prove fatal if we let it.

Get ready to stand up ... before no votes matter.

William "Jack" Hamilton is a Vic Rawl campaign aide and adviser.

IN HIGH SCHOOL, THEY CALLED HIM "TURTLE" BECAUSE HE WAS SO SHY.

TURTLE! TURTLE! TURTLE! TURTLE!

WITH HIS MOTHER DEAD, HIS BROTHER TIMMY SICK WITH CYSTIC FIBROSIS AND HIS OTHER BROTHER JIMMY GROWN AND MOVED OUT, ALVIN WAS OFTEN ALONE.

CLAP CLAP CLAP CLAP

HIS FATHER WAS A BARBER AND A CLUB-OWNER. HE WANTED BLACKS TO PLAY A BIGGER ROLE IN ENTERTAINMENT AND POLITICS.

I STARTED THIS PLACE SO WE COULD HAVE A PLACE.

ALVIN DIDN'T TALK MUCH, BUT HE DID HIS HOMEWORK AND GOT GOOD GRADES. HE DIDN'T ACT UP, SO HIS TEACHERS MOSTLY IGNORED HIM.

WHERE. IS. HE?

IT DIDN'T WORK OUT.

AFTER HIGH SCHOOL, HE JOINED THE AIR NATIONAL GUARD. HIS BROTHER TIMMY DIED WHILE HE WAS IN TRAINING.

LACKLAND AIR FORCE BASE, TEXAS

1995

HE GOT ACCEPTED TO THE UNIVERSITY OF SOUTH CAROLINA IN COLUMBIA.

12

HE STUDIED POLITICAL SCIENCE...

...AND FADED INTO THE BACKGROUND.

13

18

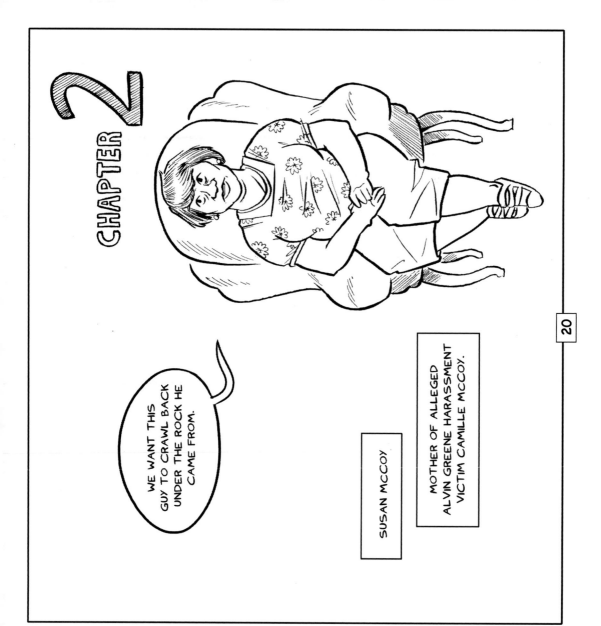

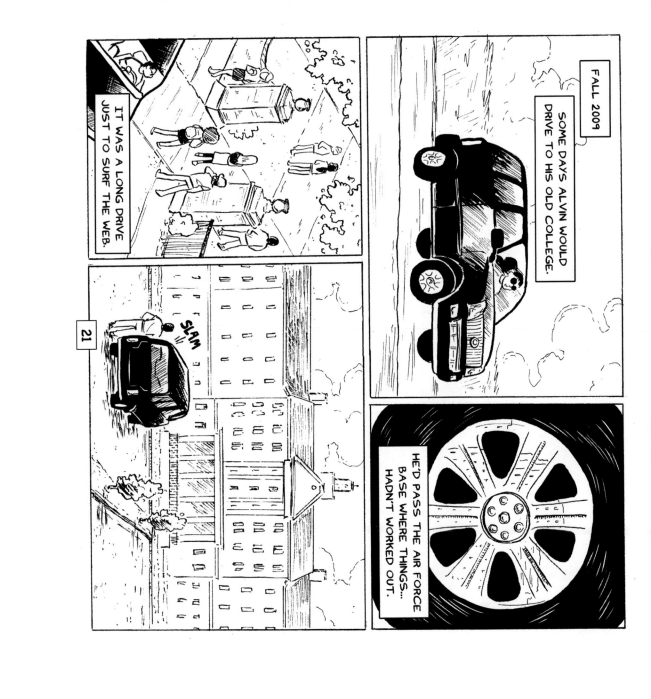

FALL 2009

SOME DAYS ALVIN WOULD DRIVE TO HIS OLD COLLEGE.

HE'D PASS THE AIR FORCE BASE WHERE THINGS... HADN'T WORKED OUT.

IT WAS A LONG DRIVE JUST TO SURF THE WEB.

SLAM

21

THIS IS WHAT HAPPENED.
ACCORDING TO UNIVERSITY OF
SOUTH CAROLINA FRESHMAN
CAMILLE McCOY.

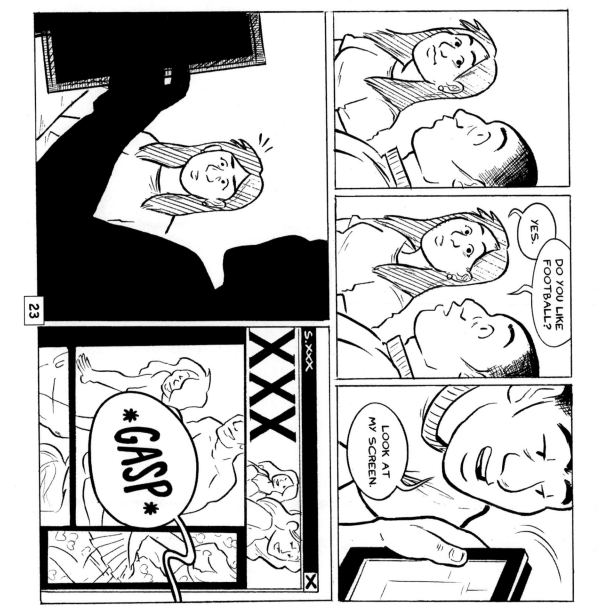

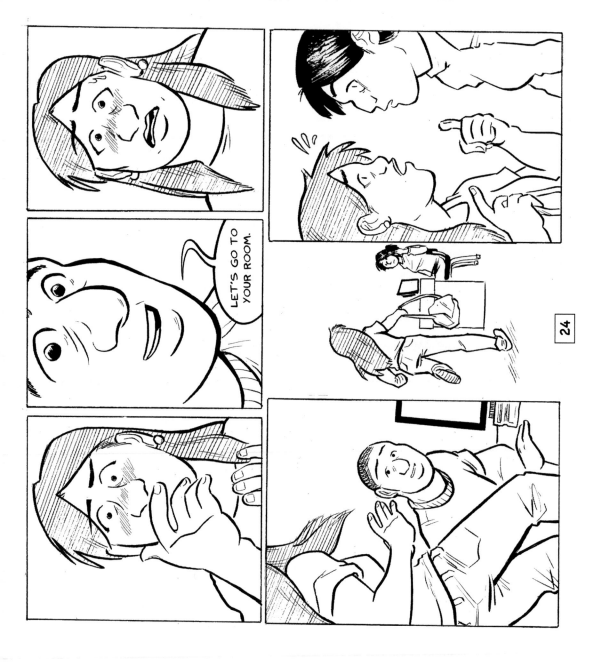

507137

BAIL WAS $500.

THE CHARGE WAS OBSCENITY – A FEDERAL CRIME.

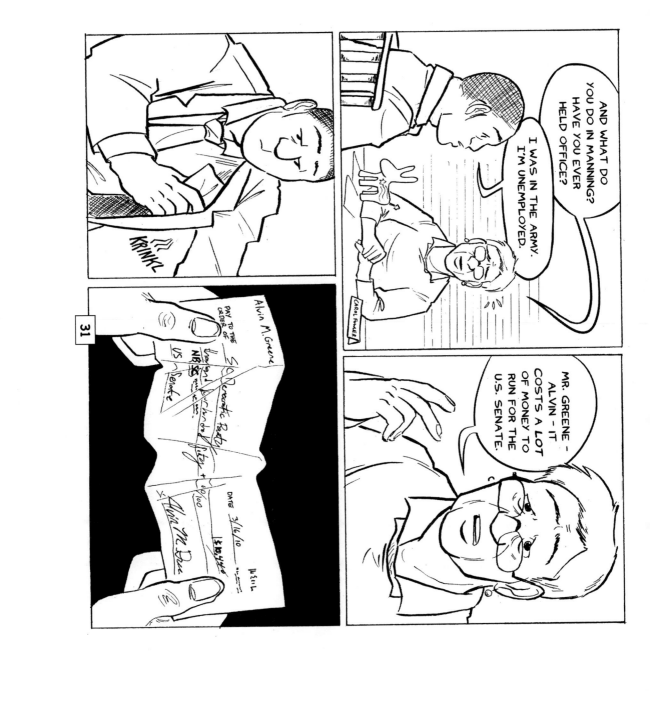

31

NOW, A
BRIEF HISTORY OF
THE TEA PARTY.

NOT *THIS*
TEA PARTY.

THE GADSDEN FLAG BECAME THE BANNER OF THE MOVEMENT.

DON'T TREAD ON ME

DESIGNED BY CHRISTOPHER GADSDEN IN THE 1700S, THE FLAG GREW OUT OF THE REVOLUTIONARY HISTORY OF CHARLESTON, SOUTH CAROLINA.

SOME CALLED THE TEA PARTY A MODERN POPULIST MOVEMENT.

LORE HAS IT THAT GADSDEN HAD BEEN ABLE TO SKILLFULLY MANIPULATE THE PASSIONS AND RESENTMENTS OF COLONIAL CHARLESTON'S WORKING PEOPLE TO SUPPORT THE POLITICAL GOALS OF THE WEALTHY AND ELITE MERCHANT AND PLANTER CLASS.

OTHERS SAID WEALTHY LIBERTARIAN POWERBROKERS HAD BANKROLLED AND STOKED THE MODERN MOVEMENT TO PROTECT THEIR CORPORATE INTERESTS.

41

The New York Times

NEW YORK Friday, April 2010

Poll Finds Tea Party Backers Wealthier and More Educated

IN THE SPRING OF 2010, A *NEW YORK TIMES*/CBS POLL FOUND THAT 18 PERCENT OF AMERICANS IDENTIFIED THEM-SELVES AS SUPPORTERS OF THE TEA PARTY MOVEMENT.

IN SOUTH CAROLINA, THE PERCENTAGE WAS MORE LIKE HALF, ACCORDING TO A WINTHROP UNIVERSITY POLL OF LIKELY VOTERS.

JIM DEMINT WAS THEIR HERO.

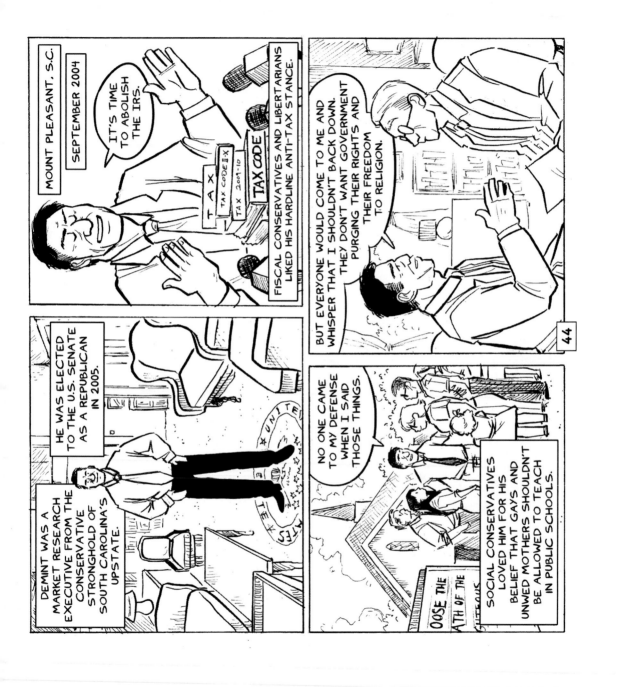

THE SEX SCANDALS OF SOUTH CAROLINA GOVERNOR MARK SANFORD AND NEVADA SENATOR JOHN ENSIGN, BOTH MEMBERS OF THE FELLOWSHIP, INVITED UNWELCOME SCRUTINY OF THE GROUP.

JOURNALISTS CRITICIZED THE FELLOWSHIP FOR USING RELIGIOUS PIETY TO COVER UP THEIR POLITICAL MALFEASANCE AND PERSONAL FAILINGS.

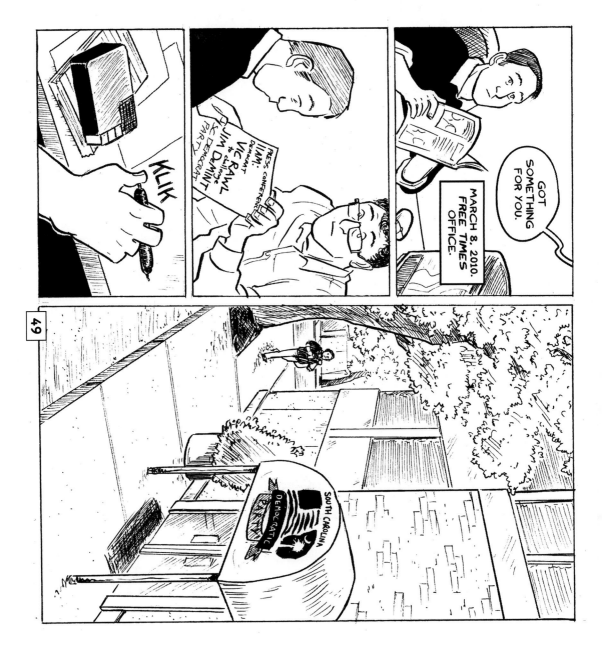

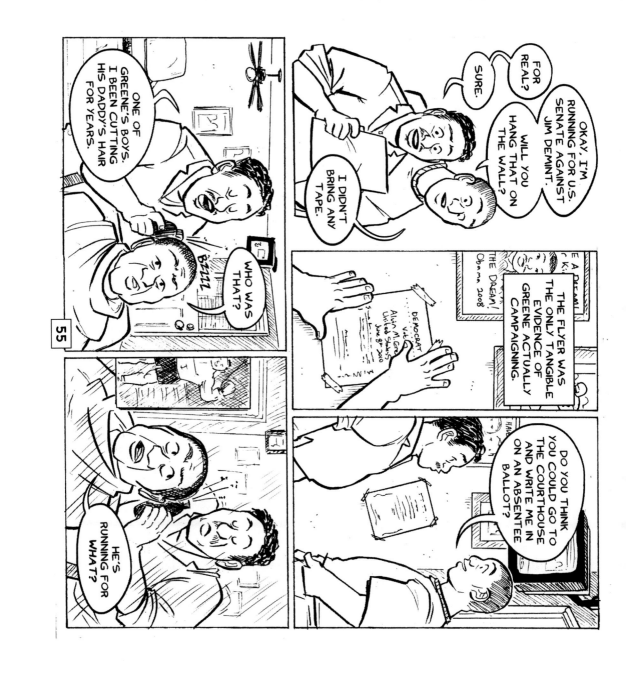

55

57

58

61

65

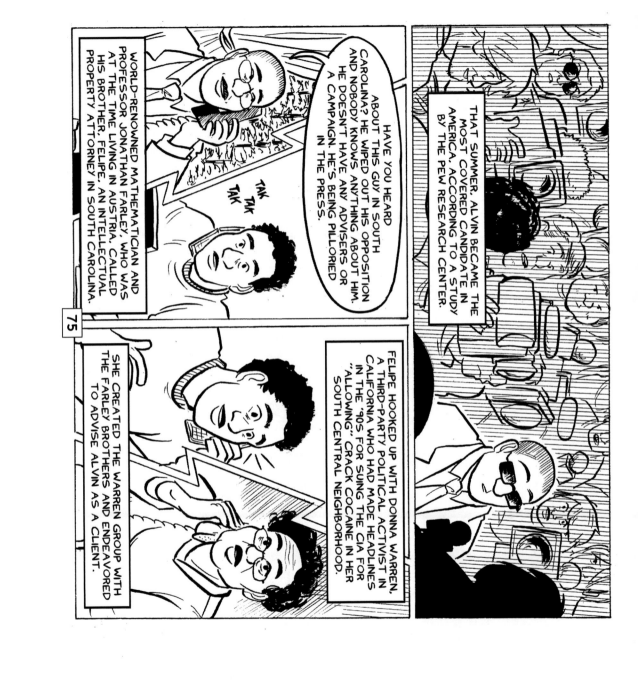

THAT SUMMER, ALVIN BECAME THE MOST COVERED CANDIDATE IN AMERICA, ACCORDING TO A STUDY BY THE PEW RESEARCH CENTER.

HAVE YOU HEARD ABOUT THIS GUY IN SOUTH CAROLINA? HE WIPED OUT HIS OPPOSITION AND NOBODY KNOWS ANYTHING ABOUT HIM. HE DOESN'T HAVE ANY ADVISERS OR A CAMPAIGN. HE'S BEING PILLORIED IN THE PRESS.

TAK TAK TAK

WORLD-RENOWNED MATHEMATICIAN AND PROFESSOR JONATHAN FARLEY, WHO WAS AT THE TIME LIVING IN AUSTRIA, CALLED HIS BROTHER, FELIPE, AN INTELLECTUAL PROPERTY ATTORNEY IN SOUTH CAROLINA.

FELIPE HOOKED UP WITH DONNA WARREN, A THIRD-PARTY POLITICAL ACTIVIST IN CALIFORNIA WHO HAD MADE HEADLINES IN THE '90S FOR SUING THE CIA FOR "ALLOWING" CRACK COCAINE IN HER SOUTH CENTRAL NEIGHBORHOOD.

SHE CREATED THE WARREN GROUP WITH THE FARLEY BROTHERS AND ENDEAVORED TO ADVISE ALVIN AS A CLIENT.

SIX DAYS AFTER ALVIN WON, VIC RAWL SAID HE WOULD FORMALLY PROTEST THE RESULTS OF THE JUNE 8 DEMOCRATIC PRIMARY.

THERE IS A *CLOUD* OVER TUESDAY'S ELECTION. THERE IS A CLOUD OVER SOUTH CAROLINA THAT AFFECTS *ALL* OF OUR PEOPLE - DEMOCRATS AND REPUBLICANS, WHITE AND AFRICAN-AMERICAN ALIKE.

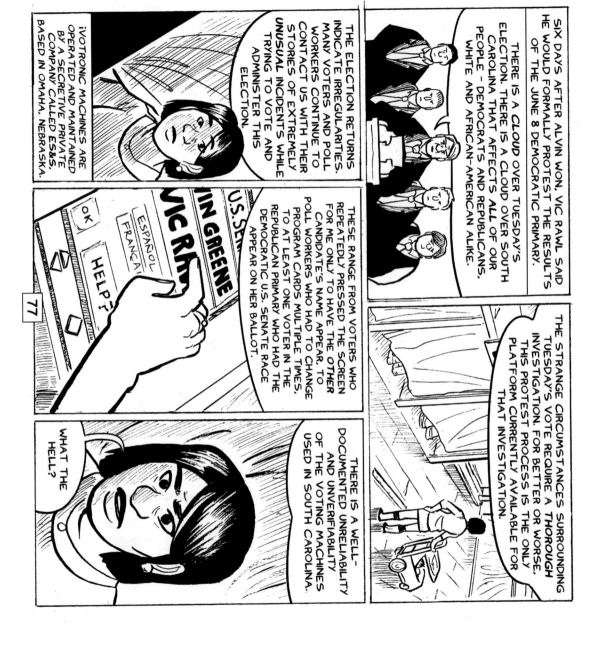

THE STRANGE CIRCUMSTANCES SURROUNDING TUESDAY'S VOTE REQUIRE A *THOROUGH* INVESTIGATION. FOR BETTER OR WORSE, THIS PROTEST PROCESS IS THE ONLY PLATFORM CURRENTLY AVAILABLE FOR THAT INVESTIGATION.

THERE IS A WELL-DOCUMENTED UNRELIABILITY AND UNVERIFIABILITY OF THE VOTING MACHINES USED IN SOUTH CAROLINA.

THE ELECTION RETURNS INDICATE IRREGULARITIES. MANY VOTERS AND POLL WORKERS CONTINUE TO CONTACT US WITH THEIR STORIES OF EXTREMELY *UNUSUAL* INCIDENTS WHILE TRYING TO VOTE AND ADMINISTER THIS ELECTION.

THESE RANGE FROM VOTERS WHO REPEATEDLY PRESSED THE SCREEN FOR ME ONLY TO HAVE THE *OTHER* CANDIDATE'S NAME APPEAR, TO POLL WORKERS WHO HAD TO CHANGE PROGRAM CARDS MULTIPLE TIMES, TO AT LEAST ONE VOTER IN THE REPUBLICAN PRIMARY WHO HAD THE DEMOCRATIC U.S. SENATE RACE APPEAR ON HER BALLOT.

iVOTRONIC MACHINES ARE OPERATED AND MAINTAINED BY A SECRETIVE PRIVATE COMPANY CALLED ES&S, BASED IN OMAHA, NEBRASKA.

WHAT THE HELL?

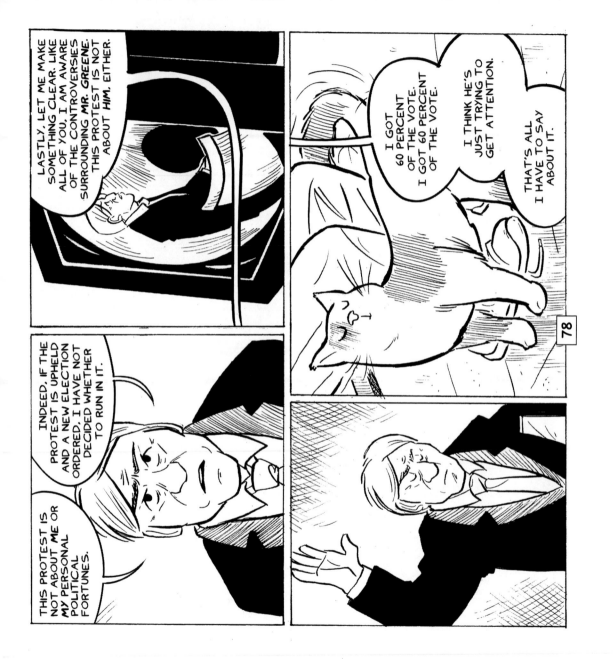

VIC RAWL GOT HIS PROTEST ON A STEAMY HOT DAY IN MID-JUNE, 2010, A WEEK AFTER LOSING TO ALVIN GREENE.

THE HEARING BEFORE THE SOUTH CAROLINA DEMOCRATIC PARTY EXECUTIVE COMMITTEE HAD THE FEELING OF A SLOW SOUTHERN TRIAL. ALVIN, OR ANY REPRESENTATIVE FOR HIM, DID NOT ATTEND.

WE BELIEVE THIS ELECTION MISFIRED. WE JUST THINK THE RESULTS ARE WRONG.

RAWL'S CAMPAIGN MANAGER, WALTER LUDWIG, TESTIFIED THAT RAWL HAD MOUNTED AN "EXHAUSTIVE CAMPAIGN."

RAWL HELD 80 POLITICAL EVENTS, LOGGING MORE THAN 17,000 MILES ON THE CAMPAIGN CAR. HE SENT 200,000 EMAILS AND MADE THOUSANDS OF PHONE CALLS. GREENE, ON THE OTHER HAND, HADN'T GIVEN A SINGLE SPEECH.

82

WHEN I PRESSED "RAWL," IT CHOSE "GREENE!"

RAWL'S NAME WASN'T EVEN ON MY BALLOT!

AS THE OFFICE MANAGER FOR THE CAMPAIGN, I CAN TELL YOU WE GOT SEVERAL EMAILS FROM VOTERS WHO HAD SIMILAR PROBLEMS AT THE VOTING BOOTH.

YOU SEE?

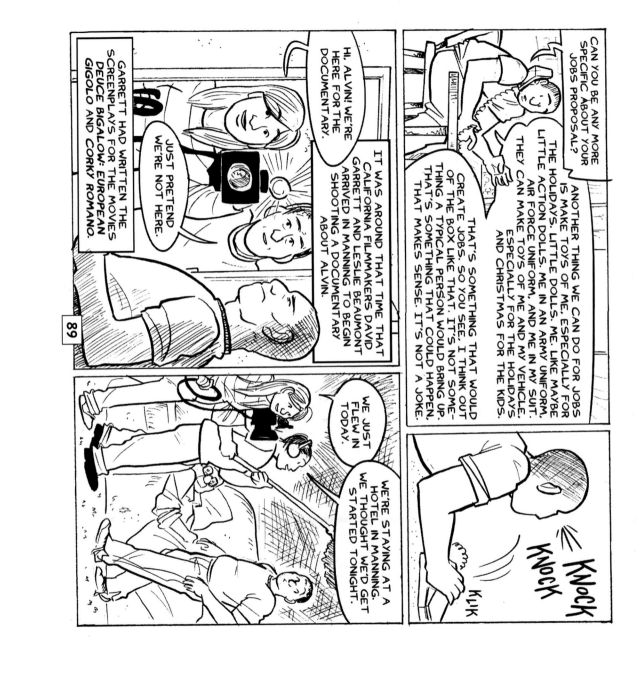

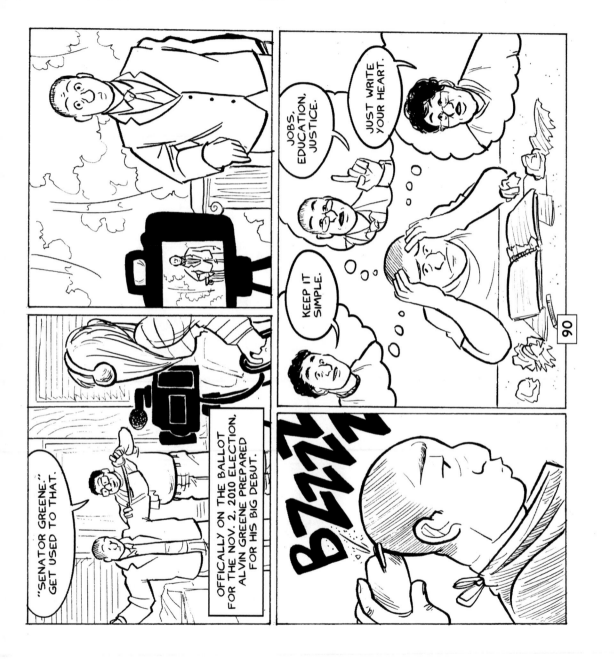

JULY 18, 2010

MANNING JUNIOR HIGH SCHOOL

MANNING
NAACP WE
ALVIN GR

GAS
GAS

SOMEONE GAVE ALL THESE YANKEES THE WRONG DIRECTIONS. KEEP COMIN' HERE ASKIN' HOW TO GET TO SOME BIG SPEECH. WHAT'S ALL THIS ABOUT, ANYWAY?

24/7

THE WARREN GROUP FACILITATED ALVIN GREENE'S OFFICIAL CAMPAIGN ROLLOUT FOR THE GENERAL ELECTION AGAINST JIM DEMINT. THE EVENT DREW PRESS FROM AS FAR AWAY AS LONDON.

ON NOV. 2, 2010, ALVIN GREENE WAS FOURTH IN LINE AT HIS LOCAL PRECINCT. HE VOTED ON ONE OF THE VERY MACHINES THAT HAD THREATENED TO TAKE HIS HIS-TORIC NOMINATION AWAY ONLY MONTHS BEFORE.

OKAY, NO. MY PARTY'S GOING TO BE BIGGER. CNN IS COVERING IT.

HE'D OPTIMISTICALLY RENTED A LARGE BANQUET HALL FOR HIS VICTORY PARTY IN MANNING.

GREENE SEN...

HE WENT HOME. WATCHED TV ALONE AND FIELDED CALLS FROM REPORTERS.

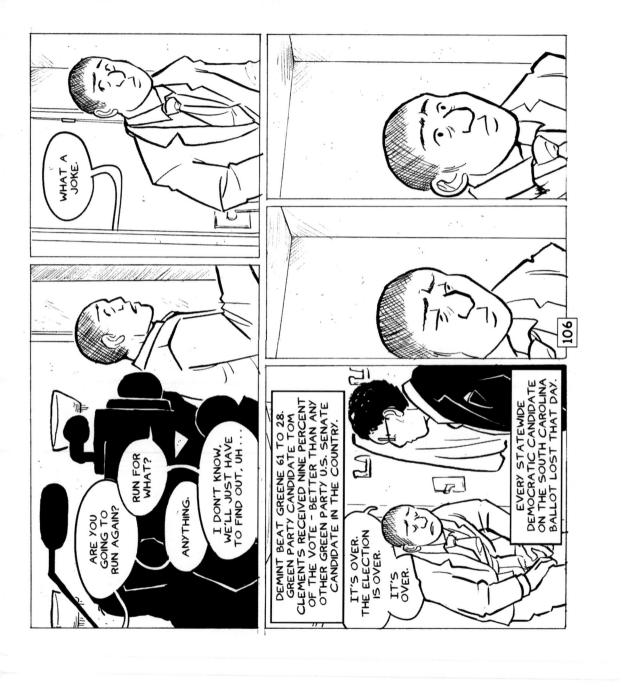

SHOULD I TELL THEM NOW THAT I'M SERIOUSLY CONSIDERING RUNNING FOR PRESIDENT?

ALVIN GREENE the Ultimate Warrior

NOT EXACTLY CONCEDING DEFEAT, ALVIN UNVEILED A COMIC BOOK THAT FEATURED HIS LIKENESS. ALVIN GREENE: THE ULTIMATE WARRIOR REFRAMED PORTIONS OF HIS BIOGRAPHY.

FORECLO

INSTEAD OF BEING INVOLUNTARILY DISCHARGED FROM THE ARMY FOR INCOMPETENCE, IN THE COMIC BOOK GREENE IS PUSHED OUT FOR TRYING TO EXPOSE THAT THERE WERE NO WEAPONS OF MASS DESTRUCTION IN IRAQ.

HE'S MESSING UP THE PROGRAM.

THEN DELETE THAT PART OF THE PROGRAM.

IT'S ON THE EFFECTS OF MICROWAVE ELECTROMAGNETIC FIELD IRRADIATION ON GLIOBLASTOMA CELL LINES.

WE CAN USE THIS TO GET RID OF HIM ONCE AND FOR ALL.

AND THAT PORNOGRAPHY CHARGE? IN THE COMIC BOOK, GREENE IS SET UP BY A SHADOW GOVERNMENT FOR BEING A THREAT TO THE MILITARY-INDUSTRIAL COMPLEX. HE ALSO SAVES FAMILIES FROM FORECLOSURE.

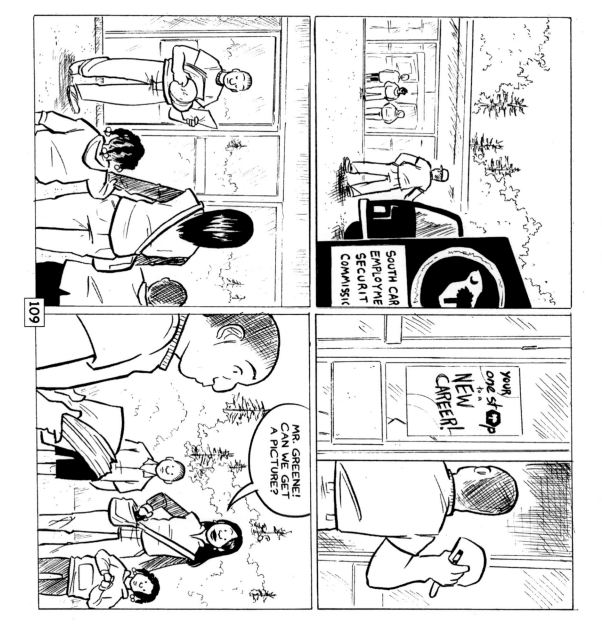

Epilogue

After Alvin Greene lost to Jim DeMint, he stayed in the newspapers for a while—mainly for flirting with the idea of running for president.

That winter, his representative in the South Carolina House, a Democrat named Cathy Harvin, unexpectedly passed away. A special election was held, and Alvin filed for the seat on Christmas Eve. He didn't campaign against his three Democratic rivals.

He lost in a landslide. Out of nearly 4,000 votes cast, Alvin Greene received fewer than 40.

That summer, prosecutors allowed him to enter a pre-trial intervention program [PTI] related to his obscenity charge.

"Mr. Greene has no other criminal record and the charge of 'communicating obscene messages to other persons without consent' is a non-violent misdemeanor, which per South Carolina statute qualifies for PTI," the solicitor said. "The charge of 'disseminating, procuring or promoting obscenity' is a non-violent felony and also qualifies for PTI; however it is not supported by the evidence and will be dismissed."

Greene maintained that he did not show pornographic images to a young woman in a university computer lab.

South Carolina Democratic Party Chairwoman Carol Fowler did not run again for the chairmanship when her term expired in 2011. Her fellow Democrats denied her a bid that year at their convention for second vice chair of the party.

Vic Rawl remains on the Charleston County Council.

William "Jack" Hamilton became active in the Occupy Wall Street movement and practices law in Charleston.

Despite a movement by some conservatives to draft Jim DeMint into the contentious 2012 Republican presidential primary, the Tea Party Kingmaker stayed out of it. He published a book that year, *Now or Never: Saving America from Economic Collapse.*

Epilogue

Filmmakers David Garrett and Leslie Beaumont fell in love while working on the documentary *Who Is Alvin Greene?* and moved in together in California. The film premiered in the summer of 2011.

In March 2012, South Carolina's longest serving lawmaker, Manning Democratic Sen. John Land, said he would retire.

Reached by phone that month at his father's house in Manning, Greene said he had no designs on the seat.

"No, I'm not gonna run for it," he said. "Nope. Nope. Nope. Nope. Nope."

It is unknown whether the cat's name really was Purr.

About the Creators

Corey Hutchins is an award-winning reporter for the Columbia *Free Times* who in 2012 was the S.C. Press Association's journalist of the year.

David Axe is a freelance war correspondent based in Columbia, S.C., and a regular contributor to Wired, AOL, Voice of America and many others. He is the author of the graphic novels *War Fix* and *War is Boring*.

Blue Delliquanti is a cartoonist who has lived in California, Massachusetts, Minnesota, Georgia, and Switzerland. She has collaborated on nonfiction graphic novels such as *Health Care Reform: What It Is, Why It's Necessary, How It Works*. Her short stories have appeared in *Womanthology* and other acclaimed comics anthologies.

Dre Lopez is a freelance illustrator in Columbia, S.C. and a founding member of Piensa: Art Company.

Index